MEANTIME

MEANTIME

Majella Cullinane

OTAGO UNIVERSITY PRESS
Te Whare Tā o Te Wānanga o Ōtākou

In memory of my mother

Dementia: from the Latin *dement*.
De-mens – out of one's mind.

—**OXFORD DICTIONARY**

She was no longer wrestling with the grief, but could sit down with it as a lasting companion and make it a sharer in her thoughts. —GEORGE ELIOT

CONTENTS

11   Memory

I. AM I STILL HERE?

15   This is not my room
16   Packing your bags
17   The believer
18   The triangle test
19   At the door
20   If the walls could speak
21   The long goodbye
22   *Embrasse-moi*
23   Sister
24   Wedding day
26   Slip
27   Sundowning

II. MEANTIME

31   All that is lost to us
32   Ice cream
33   I sleep but my heart is awake
34   A breath away
35   Interrogative
36   Ghosts
37   The number you have dialled
38   The wedding ring
39   Virtual funeral, 11 April 2020

41 These nights
42 Cut-throat
43 Meantime
45 August
46 Make no sound
48 Forget-me-not
49 Lost
50 Don't look now
51 The kind of place

III. NOWHERE TO BE

55 Anniversary
56 At your window
57 Long-distance
58 Easter
59 Small place—a haibun
60 Widower
61 Dreams
63 Winter recipe
64 Nowhere to be
65 All Souls
67 Put the heart across
68 Something to say
70 Stay here
72 The third of May
73 When I get back
74 One for sorrow, two for joy
75 In your room
78 Carried away
79 What was said
80 Notes
81 Acknowledgements

Memory

Quiver
of pīwakawaka tail
hide
and seek

scintillating waves
slick
green-blue
as kahawai

memory
slip
slips
sleuth-like
quick and shifty

Call it what you will
absent minded
forgetful
senile
the d-word
we cannot say

one day
I might
be the old woman
who doesn't remember
walking into a room
and asking—
whose memory
is this anyway?

I
AM I STILL HERE?

This is not my room

I've lost the run of myself   lost track of where I am.

I didn't know I was lost until …

     Could you take me home?

This is not my home.   This is not my room.   Someone's been in.
Someone's been wearing my shoes.   They're all out of shape.
See there—my phone's gone
and my money.   I had more than that. I'm sure.

I hear noises—
     mice scratching in the walls   trying to get out.
          Migrants are camping in the garden. The police are here again.
The other night a baby boy was born. I held him in my arms.

I want to go home now.   You can't make me stay.

I can't remember.   What was I saying?
Turn down the television.   It's too loud.
Turn off the radio.   All I want is a bit of peace and quiet—

to sleep   sleep   sleep.

Not long now until the swallows return.

The swallows will be back soon.

I can't speak.   My words are gone.   They've run away.

Am I still here?

Packing your bags

I was always the one leaving,
stretching the muscle fibres,
enlarging the chambers to fashion an octopus trap
              to break your heart.

Now it's you standing by the door
wanting to leave   wanting to go home
home   home   home.

I don't know what will get you there sooner.
You've never been the sort to give up,
even after all these years and all your talk
of some halcyon otherworld,
      the kind of place that would bore me to tears.

But go if you must. I wouldn't have you prolonged,
forget   your   name,   forget   our   names,
forget all you wish to remember.

The believer

They've been calling you more of late. They, who can't be seen or verified.
For a believer, it's hard to ignore the dead, or that other world
most can scarcely reckon with, the one you're so certain of.

Not long ago I carried my son on the back of my bike,
his voice keeping time to the path's unfolding melody.
I marvelled at the radiant peninsula stealing the light,
a sunning of cormorants unfurling their wings.

If I stay here long enough, in this place I call
my second home, this place you've never seen,
will the dead come for me too? If they send you,
you'll find me floating in the sea,
the blue sky gazing as my ears fill with water,
my limbs light and undulant,
the waves masking the sound of my last breath.

But let's suppose the dead only summon the believers,
like that child you were—walking home
with your sister from your mother's grave—
who, listening to the hum of the telegraph wire,
believed it was your mother speaking through the angels.

The triangle test

Do you remember how we cut sandwiches
into triangles when visitors came?
Ham and egg, and chicken with plenty of butter.

Did you know that there are three kinds of triangle?
No? Neither did I. Geometry was never my strong suit,
but the first instrument I played was the triangle.

Can you copy that triangle?
I wish I could have been there to give you a hint:
It looks like a mountain.

At the door

There are children playing marbles outside my door
I can hear them
                    Can't you hear them?

They belong to one of the nurses
They play marbles   all night
                I want them to stop
                                Make them stop

There's no sound at your door   there's no one at the door
           There are no players   there are no marbles
no swirling agate beating against alabaster
      no corkscrews   no ribbons nor butterflies rolling across the linoleum
no devil's eyes nor clambroths
no streaky patches of oxblood   no swirlies nor green and yellow turtles
spooling away from an ocean blue striker

I tell you about the boy I knew at school
      his nose and cheeks a constellation of freckles
the boy who beat me at marbles but who knew my favourites—
      the red-and-blue clays   the speckled cats' eyes—
           and always returned them at the end of the game

There's no sound at the door   There's no one at the door
The players have packed up
         There are no children here

If the walls could speak

what would they say? Would they remember
you asking what to do about the nightmares?

Would they hear me say
that a voice inside the dream tells me it's not real,
wakes me up before things become too frightening.

Do the walls sense you're not following,
that I must begin again, use a language you understand,
suggest you say a prayer for peaceful sleep?

When you're alone in your room, do the walls listen to your thoughts?
Do they whisper the secrets of all the old men and women
who have lain in this same bed, gazed at this same ceiling,
          counting shadows as the hours passed?

Whenever someone died, did the walls
hope someone would remember
          to open the windows to let the spirit out
and, two hours later, close them so it can't re-enter?

What if no one opened that window? What if
all those spirits were still trapped inside this room
with nothing to do but listen to you talking to them?

The long goodbye

They call what's happening the long goodbye—
this disease that each day snatches parts of you

and scatters them about, until you can't find them,
until you don't remember losing them.

You were never good at saying goodbye.

Every time I left, you hugged me
in the kitchen or the porch. You couldn't bear

to see a taxi take me away. You never stood
at a train or bus station and watched me leave.

Every time I left, you asked when I'd be back.
At the end of every phone call

you'd say *bye, bye, bye, bye for now*
and then you'd think of something else to say

and begin again our long goodbye—*bye, bye, bye, bye for now.*

Embrasse-moi

I couldn't tell you your angel's name,
but you said he was French. Angels I've heard of—
Gabriel, Michael, Raphael, the iniquitous Lucifer
        with too much time on his wings—
but let's not get into the war between heaven and hell.
That's not what this is about. For the sake of argument,
let's call yours Jean-Paul. He wore white of course.
No need to bring in feathers just yet.

Do angels fall in love?

        I don't know.

Of course not, don't be daft.

I never met your French angel who one night
slipped through the windows of a suburban rest home
to comfort fearful souls, as shadows
snooped in the dark, threaded through marble corridors, tapped
at the pipes, made them shriek like the damned.
        He dropped a few feathers,
stowed his wings under one of the old nuns' beds,
thought, *They'll never look for them there.*

Did you impress him with a few words *en français*?
Is that why he decided to linger, reminding you
it's only natural to forget who we are.
En vérité Madame, I couldn't tell you
                if I'm man or angel half the time.

Sister

I was the standby, the understudy learning the script
for the few weeks when I'd be able to step in.

I was not the one who took her to hospital
where for days she lay on a trolley waiting for a bed.

I was not the one calming her,
telling her there was no danger

while the fluorescent light resisted sleep
as much as she did.

I was not the one
who took her to appointments:

What's your address? What year is it?
Can you fold this piece of paper?

I was not the one
who took her for tea and cake afterwards

as she'd taken us to Catherine Street
every year on our birthdays.

Faithful daughter. Steadfast, like Cordelia,
despite your rantings, your follies.

Wedding day

You gaze at your wedding day photograph,
tell me you don't remember.

Thirty-four years old, you're standing next to my father,
the two of you smiling. Two years later, I was born.

Your hair turned grey, you lost most of your teeth. I don't say this.
There are other things I could say, things you wouldn't like me to mention,

about second choices, other lives left behind. I have no right.
I offer the few details you've told me down the years.

The date: April 28th, 1972. I give you a grand, soft day
with a hint of rain. The air warm, the bees buzzing as the photographer

tells you to hold still. I don't mention your niece, the dark-haired
flower girl in your wedding album at home, how she's middle-aged

and white-haired now, or the puckered face of your long-dead aunt
in an elegant navy suit and hat, who disapproved of my father.

You wore a size 8 dress. You left the convent skin and bone. All right,
I know I'm teetering; I won't mention that either, or that your father

didn't walk you down the aisle. Your eldest sister bought the garish
bridesmaids' dresses. Another sister sewed

your nightgowns together as a joke. You didn't marry in your parish church;
it was closed for repairs. When I was a child I asked you why

I wasn't there. Your attention drifts. Is some part
of you remembering as you stare at that image, or is the chasm

between the things I tell you insurmountable? The shadows
in the cave are quivering, the flames dying down. The story's

coming to an end. One more thing I've only just remembered—
the day after, you placed your wedding bouquet on your mother's grave.

Slip

Time slip—
you've returned
to the house on the corner
where we lived, years ago.

We nuzzle your neck.
Whenever we fall, you patch our knees,
wipe our tears, send us away
with a kiss.

Time slip—
let me take your hand.
Let's stay
in that home
where you find yourself
more and more, the house where

I know nothing yet
of continents or hemispheres,
of Pleiades or Matariki,
of seven daughters separated from their mother
by hundreds of light years.

Sundowning

After 'Clenched Soul' *by Pablo Neruda*

The day settles into a hazy blue dusk.
Shadows lengthen, restless trees cease their twitching.
As light submits to darkness you stare
at your reflection in the window.
Do you ask her who she is?
Does she answer?

Words plucked from your tongue,
your thoughts stumble and cower as darkness descends.

I thought we'd have more words,
or that I might sleep next to you one last time,
as I did when I was a child, our breaths
and dreams passing between us like offerings.

Together we could push back the night,
be two frightened children holding each other's hand,
walk the path between memory and forgetting,
where no sundown could ever touch us.

II

MEANTIME

All that is lost to us

Tell me your news
you whispered
over the phone … your last words to me.
Tell me your news   when all the world is screaming
and there's no other news,

when it's all about cases
and testing and tracing,
quarantine and spikes,
flattening the curve, elimination.

There's no need for you to know.
This is not what will take you.

Fracture
            of
                      memory.

Your visions: your certainty that you've seen things
that we, the doubting Thomases, cannot.

We, who would place our fingers into the wound,
feel the space   of all that is lost to us
and still not believe.

Ice cream

In my palm, three silver coins,
enough to buy three vanilla cones:
white curlicues, elaborate cloud formations,
the squeeze of raspberry syrup,
a trail leading to a snow-tipped, sugary peak.

Every Thursday, late night opening,
the three of us sat in the local shopping centre
eating our ice creams,
licking the chilly whiteness,
two girls and their mother
chatting about who knows what.

The day before you died, my sister held
a spoon of ice cream to your parched lips.
On the tip of your tongue, cool sweetness,
the three of us wiping our sticky mouths and smiling.

I sleep but my heart is awake

Every few hours, the care workers turned you.
You were struggling to breathe. They brought oxygen

but it was too late. Always impatient to be on your way
you couldn't wait for your daughter to say goodbye.

When they phoned her, they didn't say you'd already gone
or that the expression on your face was surprise

as though you'd have liked to have said—*Ah, so this is how it is*.
A pause in the rain. The robin's song soothes the morning air.

A breath away

I'll never know what your first word was.
I don't even know mine.
Did I ever ask you?

I'm sitting at the outside table.
The day is on the knife-edge of winter.
Last week a gale came through, stripped
the burgundy-auburn trees back to elemental,
their final word to me less than a word,
more a syllable, a gasp,
an exhalation—*Ah*.

Could it be that *ah* might say it all?
As if in our final moment
it becomes clear
that whatever was worth knowing
was always only a breath away.

Interrogative

Call me scavenger, looter,
  the hack seeking the next scoop,
  the nosy neighbour drawing
  their curtains back just a touch.

Call me witness, paralysed
  by the blood-stained road,
  the crushed metal,
  the glaring sign—
  Do not cross.

Call me grief's curator.
  This particular exhibition
  focuses on the interrogative:

Did you hold her hand?
  Was it warm or cold?
  Did you give her one last kiss?
  On the cheek or on the forehead?

Ghosts

You were born in a late spring snowfall,
the second twin. Three pounds—
not much heavier than a bag of sugar.

Your mother died in her thirtieth year.
She morphed into the black-and-white ghost
wearing a fedora who smiled on us as we practised
our piano scales. The same ghost who kept vigil
on Good Friday in your nursing home room
while you were dying.

How long for the talc scent on your skin to fade,
for you not to hear the early morning traffic?

Pines stir above the path
we walked last November.

Last night I dreamed of a fox,
its coppery face,
its honey topaz eyes.
It stalked outside my window,
scratching the frame
and snarling,
desperate to find a way in.

The number you have dialled

I press the receiver to my ear and listen
to my heart's hollow pulse. Nothing to distil

the distance between you and me. Curtains drawn
over winter's weary face, the cat licks condensation

from the windowpane. No switchboard with plugs or cables
to connect us, no eavesdropping operator to warn

the rumour mill. If I were to dial your number,
wait for a ringtone, it's not your voice I would hear.

The wedding ring

My sister removed your grandmother's wedding ring, gripped
your calloused palm, took your cold hand in hers,
the same hands that held us, the arthritic fingers
that once kneaded bread, the long fingers that never glided
across a piano keyboard, never strummed the strings of a guitar.

Virtual funeral
11 April 2020

Press the PLAY button of absence

First video:
You are laid out in your room at the nursing home.
You're wearing a baby blue cardigan. You're draped
with a white duvet and a purple sash.
Your skin is pale, your mouth just a little open.
I can almost hear you say
I better close it before I catch flies.
A candle on the bedside table. On the bed
three soft toys—two bears, and a piebald pig
that your grandson sent you one birthday.
Around your neck, a blue and white scarf.

Press the PLAY button of absence

Second video:
You are in your coffin. Your face is subtly made up.
Your expression is severe.
On any other day, I might have wondered
what it was that grieved you.
Again, you're wearing a scarf.
This time it's purple. I ask my sister
about the scarves. She says, *Oh, you know
what she was like about her neck.*

Press the PLAY button of absence

Third video:
A grey morning. Your neighbours stand
six feet apart on the street, paying their respects.

The hearse drives past your house one last time,
turns, waits behind two cars at the traffic lights.

Press the PLAY button of absence

I have no image of you being lowered into the ground.

On the morning of your burial, it's late evening here.
Everyone's in bed, the house is quiet.
I'm in the sitting room, lying on the couch,
waiting for the call from my sister.
She tells me she feels better now that you are safe.

Press the PLAY button of absence

These nights

What of the cicadas
singing outside the window
these last two nights
or the dream
where I didn't have the heart
to tell you
that you were dead?

Cut-throat

I could almost believe you were still here were it not for this hawthorn leaf chafing
      my trachea,
           the swell of thorny prickles in my glottis,
                clutching my throat like the rough hand of an assassin,
                    the clamped air in my windpipe, the scald of breaths
as the brain brawls for air, shrill and sharp. The neck of a bottle
      comes to mind, turning the cork to release the pressure.
           Inside, a secret message that exhales a sweet odour.

                If I cut the tree I might invite misfortune.
Wasn't it hawthorn that marked the door to the underworld?
      But that is not where I would find you.
          Haunting an old church, more like—
                standing in front of St Blaise, the Armenian martyr,
your head thrust back as he blesses your throat with a crossed candelabrum,
      your elbow nudging me, your eyes that would be saying
          What are you waiting for?

    The burst of white hawthorn petals on my tongue.

Meantime

I wake to howling wind and rush of rain.
There's talk of death and masks and distancing.
It's a year and a half since I last saw you.

The korimako darts through poroporo, striking the wet air with song.
My tongue burns. If I were to walk through autumn's cool air
I would find no relief.

I would compress seas and oceans, turn hemispheres upside down
to believe what has happened has not happened.

Reaching the halfway point of life
I recall all my days and how I have squandered them.

The rhododendron's pink blush brightens the garden,
but it has come too soon.
It will not survive early winter frosts, the Antarctic-tinged air.

The cat spends hours at the foot of the bed, asleep.
I listen to the hum of the heat pump,
to my son rifling through boxes of Lego.
Clouds drift over pines and macrocarpa.
The trees are dark green dresses swaying in the wind.
A lace of raindrops hangs on the clothes rack.

Is it any surprise we have so much locked inside us?

The dead are carried in trucks through villages.
Sands are pierced with thousands of crosses, funeral pyres burn.
A man   a woman   a child   struggle to breathe.

Death is a shared language.

I try not to think of you in the spring-churned earth, far away—
so cold in there   so cold.

Soon Matariki and her daughters will wake and pulse in the sky.

August

It doesn't matter how far away I am.
I am nothing to this place.
It cannot hold me.
The blackbird singing in the pitched edge
of darkness
will not remember me.
The yellow spark of broom that I passed
in the alleyway will not remember me.
The moon illuminating the living room
will not remember me,
cannot see the house's sleeping occupants,
or their dreams that peep through keyholes
trying to pluck themselves from the thread of loss.
Come morning, a spider's web tangled
in the clothes rack is a gift.
Later, reading an email from Inis Mór,
I imagine the Atlantic,
see hefted waves against cliffs,
grief momentarily suspended.

Make no sound

Just as, without a word, a shamed child stands with eyes fixed on the ground, acknowledging its fault while listening repentant, I stood there and made no sound.
　　　　　　　　—DANTE, 'PURGATORIO, CANTO XXXI'

I preferred the gooseberries prickling my skin to the burn of her palm.
Defiant, we looked at each other, her eyes flaring
a tawny anger, mine dark brown. On that day, my name
in the air as she called again and again for me to come out.

What did she whisper as her last breaths slackened,
till she was gone. I'd have her speak to me now—
unlock her lips, speak, speak my name into the gulf
of all that is strange and impossible, stand with me
here on this spring day and admire the cherry blossoms,
branches pouring tiny echoes over daisies on the lawn.

On my tongue, a burning, grief lodged in the throat
like an ancient cairn signposting her parting.
Could I breathe deep enough for two, smell the rain
on the air, it'd take us back for an instant, to me hiding
in those gooseberries; I would emerge gladly,
accept any punishment or rebuke. We could stay there
until some other memory came to her,
watching my small chest expand as a child, placing
her index finger under my nose to safeguard my breathing.

Light through the wind, unveil yourself, show me
your mouth arched in a smile or scowl. Speak plainly,
stockpile your convolutions, answer me this question—
why are we in purgatory? Wasn't her mind purged enough,

words swallowed and trapped until her voice went dark?
Still, since we're here, I'll be that child again,
lie close to her, inhale the clean fragrance
of her soap and talc, touch the koru of her ear.
We'll rest here, make no sound
as the blackbird sings to us in the gooseberry bushes.

Forget-me-not

Talk honestly, no one else hears you, and I stay only a minute longer.
—**WALT WHITMAN**

All morning long I see you. In the hairdressers in South Ōtepoti
you're the old woman with an overgrown bouffant perm.
Your back bears the burden of years, holds up the heavens.
The hairdresser places thin rollers in your hair.
Smiling, you tell her you're meeting your grandson soon.
Later, you sit at the window of an old-style café. You watch the world
pass by, sip scalding tea from a mug, relish
the generous spread of butter on your cheese scone.
You notice a woman seated behind you, her face plastered
with makeup. You lean towards me, whisper
Mutton dressed as lamb. Still later, near New World,
there you are again, in another café, and not only you,
there are multitudes—pairs of women, their grey hair cut short,
drinking flat whites, tucking into lamingtons.
But it's not your accent I hear, the vowels too clipped, the intonation
a scale higher than we'll ever reach. Stay a while though.
No one will hear us, or notice that I'm talking to myself.

Lost

We all so willingly record our gains, until the hour that leads us into loss.
—**DANTE** *Inferno*

I am in a room that no one else knows
is there, concealed
at the end of an empty house.
A place closed in on itself,
like this grief.
I have been here before,
seen the empty desk,
watched dreams morph each night,
their endings unchanged.
Roles reversed: I am Persephone
searching for Demeter.
I wander estates at night;
behind granite high-rises,
the atmosphere brooding, apocalyptic.
There's a hand on my mouth. I'm suffocating.
I miss connections, the train or plane
that would take me back. I'm sent off course.
A road is destroyed. A bridge is flooded;
I cannot make it across.
I am so full of sleep, dread, sleep.

Don't look now

My son sings himself to sleep.
He lies on the edge of his bed
watching twilight turn to night.
If he looks long enough
into that breach
might he hold a lamp to my face
and, like Diogenes,
ask if I'm an honest woman,
if my bones and flesh
have been replaced by glass,
how long grief will hold me?

The kind of place

You had a way of looking at me,
your amber eyes taking my measure.
I've seen my son with a similar expression,
his gaze cast on a distant point in the air,
that place where all the questions we never ask
live and breathe in a pool of stillness
and the answers we seek are composed
in some arcane cypher. The kind of place
for strange goings-on—
the ghost sitting in your front porch
looking out at the street, face turned away.
Can I be sure it's really you?

III
NOWHERE TO BE

Anniversary

Pewter-grey, the sky stares blankly.
It's not time yet, it seems to say.
You and your hemisphere, always a day ahead.
Can't you wait for her ghost to catch up?
Listen a while to the tūī song, the korimako
in the neighbour's oak tree. What's the rush?
She's waiting, just as she did a year ago.

I like to think her last dream came true
and her mother came for her in that room.
Then, drifting through suburbia's grey grid,
they wandered home together
to the blackbirds foraging in the undergrowth,
to the narrow country road where my grandmother
seated her nine-year-old daughter on the back of a bicycle,
said, *It's time for us to go.*

They say that sound is the last sense to fade.
I listen again to her favourite music:
Verdi's *Nabucco*: 'Va pensiero'.
Fly, thoughts, on wings of gold …
And there she is, right on schedule, my ghostly mother
haunting the front room, in that other hemisphere,
her hand raised slightly as she directs the air like a conductor,
her body swaying, a smile on her lips.
Isn't this just beautiful? she says.

At your window

I'll be the jackdaw stalking your roof,
my blue-black wings stirring in the breeze,
my silvery eyes peering in, my beak tap-tap-
tapping on the frosted glass. *Let me in, let me in.*

The room's empty, the bed unmade.
The mattress you slept on for years is gone.
But there are signs—the rosary beads
on your bedside table, a saint on the wall,
the soft toys perched on the headboard.

The wardrobe doors are open.
Jackdaw that I am, I catch glimpses of you
in the lavender lining of a fawn-coloured coat,
the bright collar of the azure dress suit
you liked to wear to church.

There you are again, at the back of a drawer
where, jackdaw like me, you stowed
old coins, memorial cards,
broken jewellery, passport photographs.

A clamour of rooks regards me curiously.
Fellow corvid, they enquire,
*Why are you searching for the dead
through this frost-startled window?*

Long-distance

Daughter of the long-distance phone call,
I can still hear her say
Take you to pick the furthest place on the planet to live!
But now it takes you, sister, to hold
the phone to the sky, searching for a signal,
trying to find me. Satellite witness
to grief, lead me back
to the heart that once beat next to ours.

Easter

We drove towards leaden clouds hunkering in the hills,
then left the slanting rain behind. Central Otago,
a conflagration of colour: sienna, burgundy, carmine.

We followed a tapestry of fallen maple leaves
near the Arrow river. Away, and through the hours
and what they meant, I thought of you. A year gone this week.

Something like consolation in the stars,
something left of us in that dust, or for a moment
in our footfall as we pass a shivering willow tree.

Small places—a haibun

You were happier in small places. The familiar—a second skin you cultivated. You liked to sit in the front porch and watch the street. The warmest room in the house; in summer you'd leave the door open, listen to the traffic on the main road, the airy buzz of insects in the garden. I turn my chair to the window, watch the amber oak leaves quivering. Remnant of an older world, so close, so … I watch a pīwakawaka flicker in the rhododendron. Nothing new to say, little messenger. You don't need to tell me what I already know, what's happening in those bigger places we see each night on the TV. These days, I too keep to small spaces, I, who swore my life would never be so small. Maybe there's more than one way to live at any given time. I picture myself there again, sitting in that porch, the two of us looking out on the street. The gate is closed. It's raining. There's no need for us to speak.

Pīwakawaka
flickers. Autumn's amber-blue breath
succumbs to winter.

Widower

Along the flank of the old shed he treads a path each day,
dragging his feet; his joints aching and stiff. Catching his breath,
he gazes at the apple trees, their lacquered branches, their blossoms
that fill the back garden with a faint pinkness. I imagine he leaves
the back door open, just enough to hear the voices on the radio in the kitchen.
Perhaps he keeps her chair empty on the mornings he returns to bed,
for when she has a cup of tea without him. He doesn't want to be there
when she asks why he's been keeping to the house these past two years.
It might seem like nothing changes. Does he watch the sky,
chronicle its many faces, think how the rain searching him out
makes it easier to stay inside? At night, the hours stretch.
In a dream he tells her he's off to England. She'll help pack his bags,
she says, make a sandwich and a flask of tea for the bus and the ferry.
She won't be going though. She was never much of a traveller.

Dreams

I

I dreamed you were alive
and sitting in one of those chairs
in the middle of the local shopping centre.
I left you with a gift
from your grandson. By the time I got back
you'd opened it.
You said you couldn't wait
to see what was inside. So like you,
forever opening presents early.
What was inside?
What couldn't you wait to see?

II

In the Bible, Sarah
has a child at ninety.
Last night, an old woman,
I'm sure was you,
held out her arms
and offered us the baby girl
she was cradling.

III

I heard a knocking on the front door.
Too tired to stir, I wondered,
was it you standing out there?

IV

There you lay, propped up on pillows
beneath the narrow window in our bedroom,
the same window that on windy nights frames
pulsing kōwhai shadows on the wall. You were younger
than when I last saw you. Middle-aged, your hair styled
in that tight helmet perm that was once all the rage.
You smiled, asked me where you were.
Although it has been years since I believed,
without hesitation I said, *Heaven*.

Winter recipe

You could make soda bread in your sleep.
A solemnity to your face, you'd pour flour
into a bowl, inexact splashes of buttermilk,
add a few teaspoons of baking soda
for tartness. You'd knead the dough,
shape it into a circle, cut a cruciform into the surface.
Bless the bread, Lord, and let the devil out.

From the dark hall I see your ghost
standing at the kitchen table.
Your hands are dusty with flour, your sleeves rolled up.
You ask me how my day has been.
What do I say on this first day of winter?
I watched two pihipihi fly into a sunlit tree,
a tūī sip water from the neighbour's eave.
I walked to a local bay and barely noticed the ocean.

Halfway through the year, so much unchanged.
Still, time etches deeper into our bones. The other night
there was a blood moon, the first in forty years,
and it got me counting. Will I be here for the next one?
You chuckle at my question, tell me I think too much,
that I've always thought too much, that I have no faith.

You bend your knees, place the bread in the oven,
wipe down your apron. I leave you in the kitchen,
return to my winter wanderings in the salt-tinged air.

Nowhere to be

I want to be part of that world again,
no more than a few doors on a suburban street,
the gate open, the garden with its patch of green,
the red roses dozing outside the front porch. At dawn,
the cooing pigeons, the crows catastrophising
on the shed wall. Yes, yes, I'd tell them, I've heard,
the world is nothing like it was. I'd leave the traffic hum
to the main road, mute the ticking traffic lights, silence the clock
that chimes each quarter hour outside the pub.
I'd stand outside the house that was once my whole universe.
At first, I wouldn't say a word. I'd see you
in that stirring behind the curtains, almost as imperceptible
as an intake of breath. I'd tell you I was back, that it wasn't too late,
that there was nowhere else I needed to be.

All Souls

A ghost may come; for it is a ghost's right ...
—**W.B. YEATS**

Climb inside November's flimsy veil,
burrow into that place only ghosts can see,
as obscure to us as certain shades of blue-green light
or the notes in a fragrance we can't unravel.

Think of all the things we've surrendered
for this version of ourselves. We are more
like ghosts than we'd care to admit,
uneasy in our in-betweenness.

Witness that plane in the blue sky—
a rare sight these lockdown days. Watch bees drift
from hyacinth to buttercup to marigold,
the almost indetectable tremor
of a fading kōwhai, its dull yellow flowers.
Listen to seagulls quarrelling.
Can you make out what they're saying?

I stand between the world of dream
and a morning already long awake.
Yes, I hear you. You'd have me say a prayer,
light a candle to remember the dead,
for your soul, for all the souls that linger here, or there.

This white-grey light is insubstantial, vague.
There's a stillness to the air. The church bell chimes. Seven,
the same number as the house you lived in for decades.

If you wonder why no one recognises you
since you were last there, this feeling will soon pass.
If all else fails, ring the doorbell. Ring it long and be insistent.
It's hard for your husband to hear it over the TV,
the blaring radio, the din of loneliness.

Dear soul, all souls, come in, come in.
There's no need for you to say a word.
Words are seldom useful here.
We'll take the swift impression, the feeling of déjà vu,
the candlelight mysteriously extinguished.

Put the heart across

If I said
there were times

you put the heart
across me

would you know
what I was talking about?

Something to say

I

I spent half my life telling you,
drumming it home, drilling it into your brain.
As dogmatic as any missionary
I'd cite your wrongs, list your faults,
tell you I didn't believe in your God.

Only the lighting of candles felt fundamental.
In those flickers, I saw our forebears
threading through forests after dark,
counting trembling shadows on church walls.

II

I hurt you again and again.
I did not see the ten-year-old
bequeathed such loss.

How long does it take to learn that we are all broken?

III

Take my treachery, all my so-called certainty.
I cannot forget. I ask for absolution.

IV

I'm no saint.
You said it.
I'd say it'd be pretty dull.
God forgive you. I don't know where I went wrong.

Well, it was all a bit much.
How so?
Oh, you know: the rosaries, the holy hours,
the daily Masses during Lent, the guilt,
the shame, the Apostolic church—all of it really.
But you turned out all right, didn't you?
I suppose so. As well as can be expected.
Tell me now, what's all this about?
I'm only trying to remember you.
Didn't I tell you not to? Didn't I say I'd haunt you
if you wrote about me?
You did, but you always said I was disobedient.
Never a truer word.
Still, you'd have me write a few words about you—
something to say you were here?
I might and I mightn't. If I said no,
would it make an iota of difference?
How many times have I told you?
You're not to be telling people.

Stay here

Could I tell you of tonight's stillness,
how twilight glowed behind the hills,
how a half-moon hung in a sapphire sky,
how there was not one leaf-flicker on a tree?

Could I tell you I binge-watched TV programmes
set at home (can I still call it that?),
how I yearned for my country's familiar cadences?

Could I tell you how I waited in all day,
until something shifted in me, something
I couldn't quite put my finger on?

I blew out the candle I'd lit for you.
Before I left the house, I opened the bathroom window
even though I was carrying the front door keys.
I've stopped trusting in the simple function of things.

Outside, the street was deserted.
I was alone but not lonely.
There is nothing like an autumn sky for beauty.

On the path, a girl and I exchanged smiles.
Her blue mask hung under her chin;
mine was in my shopping bag.

Could I tell you the cat followed me to the shops
but I didn't notice until I met her on the train tracks
as I was coming home? You would have laughed.

Could I tell you I wish you could see this sky?
We could sit on the deck.
Ignore the overgrown clematis—I'm not much of a gardener.
I wish I could speak to you
but I don't understand the language of the dead.

Stay here and watch with me.
Watch the sky shift from flaxen to coral to mauve
And, as the minutes pass, to muted grey.
Let's watch with the door open for the light to go.

The third of May

I walk through the old church grounds,
past bluestone walls scarred with scaffolding,
across the train tracks. The road climbs

through a canopied grove. On the hill-top,
the town's graveyard. Here I meet the dead,
decades gone, their names etched in stone.
A Moloney, a Munro, an Alexander, even a Love.

Autumn parades its flush of leaves.
Low cloud stretches across the peninsula and port.
It's your birthday today.

When I get back

I'll find your gravestone,
the black Celtic cross you chose,
your name and lifespan carved in marble.
I'll bring you the trill of blackbird song,
a grey-blue sky, the murmuring of oak trees
behind the graveyard's old stone walls.
Through the stars' fading light,
I might hear you say,
Ah, you're home now, you're home.
What took you so long?

One for sorrow, two for joy

I'd been keeping away from the reception room, as you called it,
away from the sideboard with your dusty silver teapots,
the sugar bowls and jugs I used to polish as a child,
away from the flotsam of old photographs on the piano top,
that ornament where a boy kisses a girl,
the shelves of crystal glasses and china cups you never drank from.

To draw myself in, I sit where you once sat, begin to read.
The house opposite looks on impassively as I turn the pages.
The hours move slowly, and for each minute I wait
there might be one where
I hear the front door open and close,
the rattle of your keys as you fling them on the hall table.
You call my name, say you'd love a cup of tea.

A magpie in its black and white tuxedo lands on the porch roof,
flicks its tail like a flamboyant concert pianist.
You taught me the rhyme. One for sorrow, two for joy,
three for a wedding, four to die …
How many for the red roses outside the window to unfurl?

In your room

I

The Virgin Mary's fluorescent cloak glimmers white,
the LED glows for seconds after it's switched off.

I listen for that momentary exchange in the hall,
the brush of air sifting between the stairs and the landing—

how it loses itself at the door of your room,
startled by a sliver of light through the gap in the curtains.

I fall asleep while your bedroom talks on.
My heart slows, my breath dips.

II

You are everywhere and nowhere.

Your room's been closed for nearly three years.
It still smells of you.

Cobwebs stretch across the walls
like grey alveoli.

On your windowpane
a large sticker of St Michael,
his sandalled foot crushing Satan's neck.

Then, the sound I've been waiting for.
At first, only a trace
through my pre-dawn, jetlagged stupor:
a crow, caw-caw-cawing.

III

My sleep is episodic, shallow.
I'm wearing your pastel pink pyjamas.
DREAMING OF THE WEEKEND
is splayed across the front.
The legs and arms are too short.
They're not my sort of thing.

IV

The pigeon on the roof has a lot to say for itself.

V

I rifle through drawers,
looking for a message from you.

Nothing

> to interpret this morning's flint-grey sky,
> or tell me why, as it appears, you've just absconded.

A near-empty bottle of your perfume
on the dressing table,

your walking stick in the corner, its curled hook
holding the air hostage, and that spider.

> How long has it been there?
> > Could it be in on your disappearance?

VI

I open your bedroom window,
let the air in

release

all the days
neither of us were here.

Carried away

> ... *I have pretended ease,*
> *loved with the trickeries of need, but not enough*
> *to shed my daughterhood ...*
> —ANNE SEXTON, 'THE DIVISION OF PARTS'

I open your wardrobe. Satiny linings, woollen coats,
leopard-skin prints, tweed and pinstripe jackets,
fur-lined collars, suede. I inhale your scent.

You were never one for writing, so I can't say why I inspected
your pockets for secret notes. I found tissues and rosary beads—
those shackled stones you rubbed between finger and thumb,
the three sets of five mysteries: joyful, sorrowful, glorious.
I wonder which was the last one you said? In another pocket,
a handful of loose change, scarcely enough to buy us a pot of tea.

I take one of your favourite coats, purple with four large buttons
and a wide collar. Two sizes too big. You always liked your clothes roomy.

It'll be winter when I return. I'll take you places we've never been.
No one need know I'm carrying my mother on my back,
so far from this semi-detached house, the quiet street,
        four magpies scuffling on my father's shed.

What was said

Your gravestone faces
the memorial to Independence,
the chalk-white statue
of a local hero, arm raised,
rifle slung over his shoulder.
He's wearing a long coat, a rebel's cap.

The first time I visited
       I talked to you in my head.
       I wasn't alone.

Rain swept over.
       Rooks in the trees
              jabbered relentlessly.

The second time,
I touched your gravestone,
traced your name there,
your birth year, the year you died.

       Only you know what was said.

Notes

'Packing your bags' – The phrase 'octopus trap' refers to takotsubo (or broken-heart) syndrome. In this condition, the heart's main pumping chamber changes shape, affecting its ability to pump blood effectively. The heart's chamber looks similar to a takotsubo pot, a Japanese fishing pot used to catch octopus.

'The triangle test' – The triangle test is one of many tests for dementia designed to assess memory and cognitive function.

'If the walls could speak' – Traditionally an Irish wake is held in the home of the deceased or of a close relative; known as the wake house. In the past, it would have been the front room or parlour. Immediately after death, a window was opened to allow the spirit of the deceased to leave the house. No one should stand or block the path to the window as this may prevent the spirit from leaving and will bring misfortune to the person who impedes the way. After two hours, the window should be closed so the spirit cannot re-enter.

'Sundowning' – People with dementia often become more confused and restless in the early evening. They may become more demanding, upset, suspicious, disoriented and even see, hear or believe things that aren't real, especially at night. Experts believe that 'sundowning' may relate to lack of sensory stimulation after dark. Many families and carers say that the person becomes more anxious about 'going home' or 'finding mother' late in the day, which implies a need for security and protection.

'I sleep but my heart is awake' is a line from The Song of Solomon 5:2.

'Winter recipe' – *Let the devil out of the bread.* In Munster, (south-west Ireland) soda bread is baked in round loaves with a cross cut on top of the bread. Traditionally this was done for superstitious reasons as it was believed the cross would not only bless the bread but also ward off evil. As the bread was cut with a knife, a woman might also say 'let the devil out of the bread' or, in some parts of Ireland, 'let the fairies out'. The cruciform shape of the cross is also symbolic of Ireland's Christian heritage. Practically speaking, slashing the dough also allows heat to penetrate into the thickest part of the bread in order for it to stretch and expand as it rises.

'Put the heart across' – The Hiberno-English phrase 'to put the heart across' is from the Irish *an croí a chur trasna i nduine* and means to startle or frighten someone.

Acknowledgements

I acknowledge the generous financial support from Copyright Licensing New Zealand (2020) and Creative New Zealand (2021), which enabled me to write and complete this collection. I'd also like to thank The Caselberg Trust where I spent a week in 2020 writing some of these poems.

Many thanks to Andrew Court, Rhian Gallagher and Emer Lyons for their reading of this manuscript during its many stages; to Maxine Alterio, Emma Neale, Andrea McCartney, Carolyn McCurdie, Ailbhe McDaid and Jan Redmond for their ongoing encouragement and friendship. Thanks to Sue Wootton for her assiduous and considerate editing of *Meantime*.

A very special thanks to my sister Marie Quinlivan who was, and is, always there, and to my father Michael Cullinane (1933–2022) for his love of language and history. Many thanks to the care staff at St Paul's Nursing Home in Limerick for their exceptional care of my mother; most especially in the last weeks of her life, and through the extreme challenges of the first Covid-19 lockdown of March–April 2020.

Acknowledgements are due to the editors of the following publications where several of these poems have appeared: *Poetry New Zealand* (2021), *New Zealand Poetry Society Anthology* (2021), *More Favourable Waters: Aotearoa Poets Respond to Dante's Purgatory*, edited by Marco Sonzogni and Timothy Smith (Cuba Press, 2021), *The Spinoff*, *The Otago Daily Times*, and Dunedin Public Library.

'Small places—a haibun' was Commended in New Zealand Poetry Society's 2021 International Poetry Competition.

Published by Otago University Press
Te Whare Tā o Te Wānanga o Ōtākou
533 Castle Street
Dunedin, New Zealand
university.press@otago.ac.nz
oup.nz

First published 2024
Copyright © Majella Cullinane
The moral rights of the author have been asserted.

ISBN 978-1-99-004880-7

A catalogue record for this book is available from the National Library of New Zealand. This book is copyright. Except for the purpose of fair review, no part may be stored or transmitted in any form or by any means, electronic or mechanical, including recording or storage in any information retrieval system, without permission in writing from the publishers.

No reproduction may be made, whether by photocopying or by any other means, unless a licence has been obtained from the publisher.

Editor: Sue Wootton
Cover: Shutterstock

Printed in New Zealand by Ligare